THE SUPERHEROES' GUIDE
TO DOMINATING THEIR UNIVERSE
A WORKBOOK

Aggrandize Your Life Publishing, LLC
Durham, NC

Written by San Griffin
Cover Design by Eliran Malka

All rights reserved. No portion of this book may be reproduced in any form or distributed without permission from the publisher, except as permitted by U.S. copyright law. For permission contact: www.aggrandizeyourlife.com

Edited by LaKela Atkinson and Tracie Fellers

Layout design by Garry Atkinson, Fundo Press LLC

Copyright © 2017 by Aggrandize Your Life Publishing, LLC. All rights reserved.

Library of Congress Control Number: 2017952167

DEDICATION

This book is dedicated to all of the young brilliant minds around the world. Yes, that's you! To the amazing parents, educators and youth leaders around the world, thank you for investing in your youths' mindset! Change the mind, you change the world!

Additionally, thank you to my supportive husband Milton, and our three sons for keeping me inspired.

-San Griffin,
Entrepreneur

FOREWORD

Shontè Jovan Taylor,
Neuroscientist, Entrepreneur, and Mindset Success Catalyst Trainer

"It takes courage to grow up to be who you really are."
~ EE Cummings

I have the honor of preparing young minds to receive ideas through positive affirmations that will shift their thinking for ultimate fulfillment and success in life. It takes courage to become our best selves when there are constant forces, both seen and unseen, smothering us to be average.

The sooner we start to create positive, courageous, and action-oriented mental pathways of success and growth, the sooner we can evolve to the highest version of ourselves. What better start than to teach our youth to do so. Their brains after all, are sponges and capable of unparalleled growth thus shaping their destiny.

As a Neuroscientist, Mindset Success Catalyst Trainer, entrepreneur, mother, & wife, I know the power of training our brains and minds to reach our highest levels of success, compassion, and ultimately our humanity. The affirmations in this book that you will read do just that. I ask students reading this book to be open as the author takes you on a mental odyssey of successful thinking and practice. It will be a journey of shaping the mind through harnessing and incorporating the brain's senses to ensure that the affirmations become not just words, but indelibly written in the hearts and minds of those who are willing to have the courage to BECOME. Thank you, San Griffin for having the vision to change the world in such a powerful way.

INTRODUCTION

I wrote this book looking through the lenses of an educator, a mother, a neuroscience lover, and advocate of empowerment. This workbook is vital to developing a healthy mindset in our youth; however, adults will enjoy and glean from this workbook as well.

Why have youth speak affirmations?

This book encourages positive affirmations. According to the field of psychology, positive affirmations repeated out loud to ourselves impress upon the subconscious mind to accept the idea. A recent study from a team of researchers at Carnegie Mellon University confirms that affirmations are effective.[1]

Why have them see positive images?

Additionally, as we become adults and begin our study in various fields, we learn about the term self-fulfilling prophecy – a thought or expectation manifesting in a person's life because it has been imposed on them directly or indirectly. Whether words are spoken over us or stereotypical images are all we seem to see, both are impactful. Why not have this principle work for youth versus against youth?

Why write goals?

In studying neuroscience, I learned that writing connects the conscious mind to the subconscious mind, which makes the act of writing a powerful influence.

Why meditation?

According to a Harvard neuroscience study, meditation changes the structure of the brain positively and strengthens the cerebral cortex. The prefrontal cortex is where your decision-making process is located.[2]

Actually, these principles are embedded all around the world and have been from the beginning of time. This is what inspired me to gather quotes from different cultures, and examples from well-known figures to include in this workbook.

Why wait until our youth are grown for them to stumble upon this vital information to have a prosperous, happy, intentional life. Share it now!

TABLE OF CONTENTS

MEET CREATOR JR (AKA KID UNI)	7
YOU ARE LIKE YOUR PARENTS	8
PUTTING YOUR WORDS TO WORK	9
VISUALIZATION SKILLS	10
SUPER POWERS	11
MEDITATION	12-13
LOVE	14
APPLYING WORDS CAREFULLY	15-16
PRACTICE GRATITUDE	17-18
NOW LET'S DO IT	19
LAW OF ATTRACTION	20
LEARNING STYLES	21
KNOW YOUR BRAIN	22
SET GOALS	23
THINK BIG AND DREAM	24
BE CREATIVE	25
CREATE A VISION BOARD	26
STARS WHO'VE DONE IT	27
SHINE BRIGHT	28
AFFIRMATIONS	29
SUPERHEROES' LOG	30
KID UNI'S FAREWELL	31
ABOUT THE ILLUSTRATORS	32-33
NOTES	34
ABOUT THE AUTHOR	35

CHARACTER: CREATOR, JR., AKA KID UNI

Meet Creator, Jr., also known as Kid Universe, and affectionately called Kid Uni. Kid Uni enjoys exploring, sharing, and meeting new friends.
However, he too is still learning that he has super powers. His mission is learning how to tap into his powers and recognize them to manifest the life he desires. He will go along with you on this journey of discovery as you read this workbook.

Kid Uni is well-equipped for the journey. His open cranium represents the infinite knowledge that he possesses. He is always learning and his imagination is robust!

The star on Kid Uni's chest represents the superhero status that he was born with. He is destined to be a superstar!

The padding on his outfit provides support and is extra thick to protect him along his journey. His parents knew he would need this during his escapades as he stumbles, falls, or takes risks.

The pockets represent Kid Uni's preparation, as he was told to never leave home without essentials.

Finally, the symbol on his shoes reminds him to stay focused and on the right path.

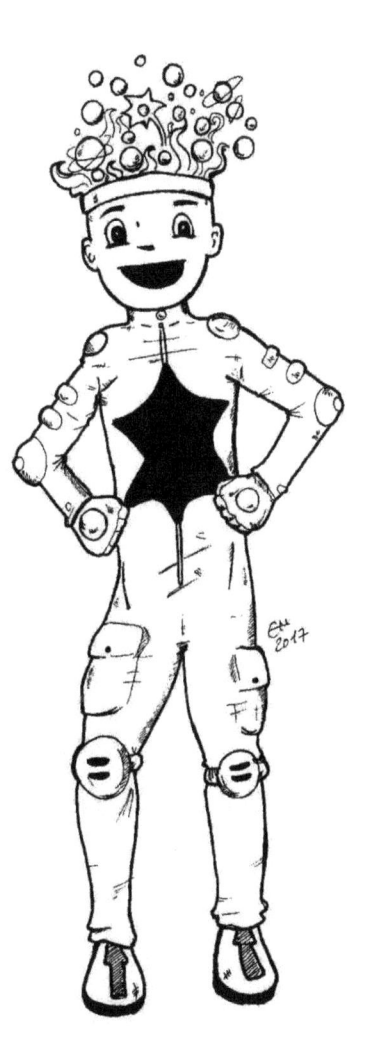

KNOW,
YOU ARE LIKE YOUR PARENTS

Have you ever heard anyone say, you are just like your father or mother"?

Well, you are! Because of DNA, you may have visible traits that are similar, such as facial features, hair color, skin color, and probably some similar personality traits and mannerisms.

GUESS WHAT?

Creator, Jr., aka Kid Uni, is like his parent, the Creator – that's right, the creator of the universe. The Creator spoke things into existence, and Kid Uni soon began speaking affirmations into his life. You and Kid Uni have a lot in common. You too can practice using your words effectively. You say things every day. Be mindful of the words you chose. Your thoughts become words, and your words become things and actions.

LIKE KID UNI, LETS START
PUTTING YOUR WORDS TO WORK FOR YOU!

Write or say three things you want to declare about yourself and/or your confidence.

1._____

2._____

3._____

For example:
 I am brave.
 I am surrounded by people who love me.
 I am a scholar.

Affirmations

"These repetitive words and phrases are merely methods of convincing the subconscious mind."

-Claude Bristol
Author

"Wherever the head goes, the tail will follow"

-Filipino Proverb

USE YOUR VISUALIZATION SKILLS

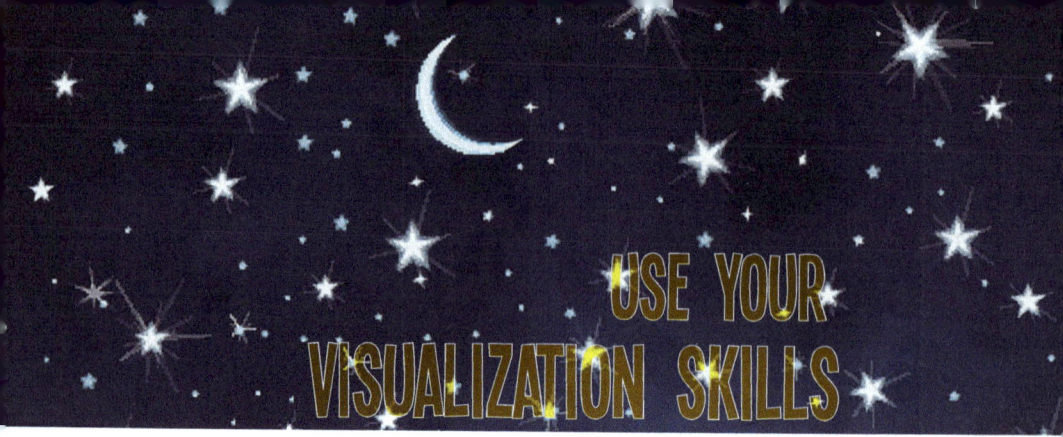

Illustration from iStock by Getty Images

Remember when you decided in your mind what you were wearing to school on the first day? You SAW it in your mind – the colors, the fit, the feel, and the cool emotions of wearing that outfit. You thought about how your friends would react to it, eyes bulging, jaws dropping, foes doing a double take when they saw you. That was VISUALIZATION.

Can you think of another time you used the skill of visualization?
What was it that you visualized?
Did it come to pass?

"Everything you can imagine is real."

-Pablo Picasso
Spanish painter

"I dream therefore I become."

-Cheryl Renee Grossman
Author

"The world belongs to those who cross many bridges in their imagination before others see even a single bridge."

-Chinese Proverb

DISCOVER YOUR
SUPER POWERS

Everyone has SUPER POWERS (including YOU), and you will discover your zone of GENIUS in due time.
You will discover it when certain things come easy and effortless for you. When you are having fun doing something that other people find difficult or not so fun, you may be on your way to recognizing your super powers.

If we took a fish out of the water and put it on the floor, it would flip-flop around. One would think,"That's a dumb old fish". But when you put it back in its element, that same fish is GENIUS. It is doing what it was created to do. It comes easy to him. What comes easy to you? Whatever it is, you are a GENIUS in
that area.

Find your ELEMENT GENIUS – and use those
SUPER POWERS!

Can you imagine if Michael Phelps was racing in the Olympics and Usain Bolt was swimming?
Get in your zone of GENIUS!

Photographs from iStock by Getty Images

PRACTICE
MEDITATION

You know how you cut off your computer, cell phone or other electronic devices so they work without slowing down or crashing? Well, your brain also needs a break so it can perform at its best when you need it to. YOUR personal computer!

So learn to UNPLUG IT sometimes.

START by sitting in a quiet space and just listening to yourself breathe in and out for about fifteen minutes during the day. Let the rhythm of your heart and breathing relax you. Try NOT to think about anything else. It will take some practice, so if hard to do at first, keep trying. Don't give up.

MEDITATION BREATHING
EXERCISE

Try this technique...
SMELL the cake
BLOW out the candles.
Do it 10 times, then 20 times
and keep going for 15 minutes
GUESS WHAT?
You've just been meditating!

Illustration from Adobe Stock

"All of man's problems stem from his inability to sit quietly with himself."

-Pascal
French mathematician, physicist, philosopher

"The more we learn to link the use of breath, mind, and voice, the greater our own power in life."

-Ted Andrews
Author

"In the midst of moment and chaos, keep stillness inside of you"

-Deepak Chopra
Author

WALK IN
LOVE

If you truly want to DOMINATE, one must master love!

Love conquers all.

How do you define love?

_____

How do you describe love?

_____

"Love is like dew that falls on both nettles and lilies."
-Swedish Proverb

APPLY
WORDS CAREFULLY

In school, you say meaningful words on purpose. These include pledges, school anthems, cheers led by cheerleaders, or chants at school games. To join most organizations or other groups, you use WORDS. You get the point?

WORDS are powerful! They can help, bully, unify, or hurt. You have the power to choose the right words to work for you.

> "Don't ever diminish the power of words. Words move hearts and hearts move limbs."
>
> -Hamza Yusuf
> Scholar

WORDS are energy you put into the atmosphere, so be careful about what you say. For example: We will lose the game tonight vs. We always win

speaking bad
+ hearing bad
= feeling bad

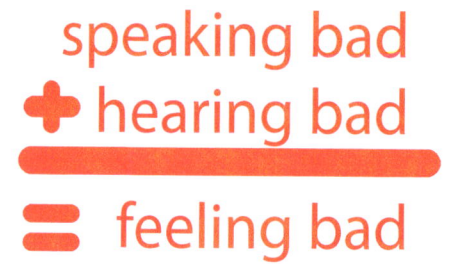

speaking good
+ hearing good
= feeling good

"Anger is as a stone cast into a wasp's nest."
-Indian Proverb

PRACTICE
GRATITUDE

Being thankful is vital! ALWAYS have an attitude of thankfulness because that creates an environment for more goodness to come. Remember, things could be worse. So say it loud. I'M THANKFUL!

Each day, write down five things you're thankful for.

1._____
2._____
3._____
4._____
5._____

"He is a wise man who does not grieve for the things which he has not, but rejoices for those which he has."

-Epictetus
Greek philosopher

"True power comes from serving and helping others."

-Dalai Lama
Leader

WHICH ROAD WOULD YOU RATHER TAKE?

DRILL IT IN
NOW, LET'S DO IT!

Most people know the principle (rule) of applying impactful words. Now, let's take action and just do it!

APPLY IT NOW. Write down four things you want to speak positively about – to affirm yourself, your personality, and your goals.

EXAMPLES:
- I AM an honor roll student.
- I AM outgoing and love meeting new people.
- I AM very healthy and happy.

1. _____
2. _____
3. _____
4. _____

I am...

amazing

intelligent

beautiful

Now, say it out loud everyday in the mirror, in the morning and at bedtime. Just make time to FRAME YOUR PATH!

UNDERSTAND THE
LAW OF ATTRACTION

You are magnetized. That means you attract what you think about the most, whether it is good or bad. So, let's think more delightful, positive, and happy thoughts.

Think BIG! If you think you can, YOU WILL! It's OKAY not to know how right now. Just believe.

Now think about it…
Are you thinking more happy thoughts or destructive thoughts?

"Whether you think you can or can't either way you are right."

-Henry Ford
Successful entrepreneur

"If you dream it, you can do it."

-Walt Disney
Successful entrepreneur

"Your imagination is your preview of life's coming attractions."

-Albert Einstein
Physicist

BE AWARE OF
LEARNING STYLES

Each of us is unique and original. We all learn and analyze things differently.

You ARE NOT slow, dumb, or stupid. It may take a little time, but you will discover your zone of genius! Until then, persist and don't give up!

Some people are:

Visual Learners
Like pictures, movies, charts & diagrams, handouts

Auditory Learners
Like music, discussions, lectures, and have a good memory

Reading and Writing Learners
Like listing, reading, taking notes, and understanding efinitions

Kinesthetic (or Tactile) Learners
Like movement, experiments, and hand-on activities

Illustrations from Adobe Stock

"Today the greatest single source of wealth is between your ears."
-Brian Tracy
Motivational Speaker

"Success is 10% ability and 90% sweat."
-Nigerian Proverb

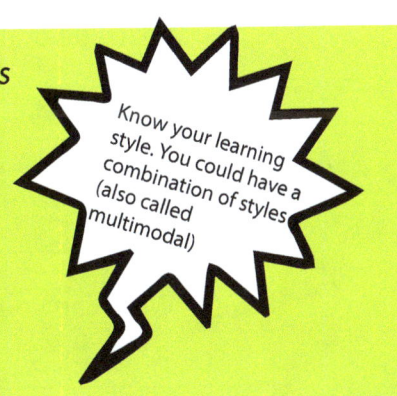

Know your learning style. You could have a combination of styles (also called multimodal)

21

KNOW YOUR BRAIN

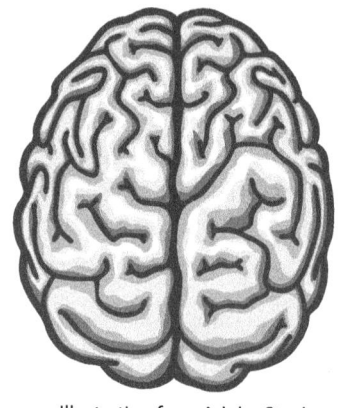

Illustration from Adobe Stock

Left brain:

Computation

Mathematics/Scientific Facts

Logic

Sequencing

Analytical Skills

Right brain:

Using Creativity

Imagination

Rhythm

Feelings

Spatial perception

Visualization

Pictures/images

What side of the brain do you think dominates in you?

_____

Why?

_____

What can you do to exercise the less dominant side?

_____

SET
GOALS

A goal is defined as something you are trying to do or achieve. Setting goals and accomplishing them will help you progress.

Set three goals

1. _____
2. _____
3. _____

Now, think: What actions do you need to take to reach these goals?

1. _____
2. _____
3. _____

When do you want to reach these goals?

1. _____
2. _____
3. _____

"Begin with the end in mind"

-Dr. Stephen Covey
Author and Educator

THINK BIG AND DREAM

Illustration from iStock by Getty Images

Explore, be curious, try new things, and go to new places. Exposure to other cultures, places, books, museums, music, and languages prepares you to broaden your scope of thinking. Fuel your BRAIN!

Believing is simply thinking something will happen. There is amazing energy surrounding the idea of believing. We do it daily unknowingly, so be purposeful about it!

Aspire to do something unprecedented. Don't limit yourself.
What are your dreams?

"Shoot for the moon, because even if you miss, you'll land among the stars."

— Les Brown
Motivational Speaker

BE CREATIVE

Use your cleverness and originality to craft, innovate, and discover new methods, interpretations, ideas, and patterns in what interests you.

Use the space below to doodle your ideas.

"Creativity is just connecting things. When you ask creative people how they did something, they feel a little guilty because they didn't really do it, they saw something. It seemed obvious to them after a while. That's because they were able to connect experiences they've had and synthesize new things."

-Steve Jobs
Inventor

CREATE A VISION BOARD

You can draw things that remind you of your goals —or gather magazines and newspapers to cut out pictures, quotes, symbols, or drawings that represent your goals and future achievements or the grades you want to make in school.

HERE'S WHAT YOU NEED:

- Scissors
- Bright stickers
- Cardboard
- Magazines and/or newsapers
- Glue
- Markers
- Construction Paper

Illustration from Adobe Stock

AND A VIVID IMAGINATION!
FOLLOW THESE STEPS:

1. Cut out the objects that symbolize your short-term (right now or near future) goals, all the way to your long-term goals (further in the future).
2. Paste them onto the cardboard or poster paper in an organized fashion that you like.
3. Hang the poster in your bedroom or somewhere you can look at it multiple times a day to keep your focus and remind you of your goals.
4. Visualize how you will feel when those goals come to pass.

STUDY
STARS WHO'VE DONE IT

- Katy Perry, an American pop star, created her first vision board when she was 9 years old. Katy has publicly shared that on her vision board, she included a picture of Selena, a popular Latin pop singer at the time. The picture depicted Selena holding her golden Grammy Award statuette. Fifteen years later, Katy was nominated for her first Grammy Award.[3]

- Michael Jordan, one the most famous athletes in the world, also utilized visualization. Jordan, aka "His Airness," stated, "I visualized where I wanted to be, what kind of player I wanted to become. I knew exactly where I wanted to go, and I focused on getting there."[4]

- Successful comedian and actor Jim Carrey is another star who used positive thinking. Carrey was once a struggling young actor. He openly acknowledged that he used visualization skills to picture himself being the greatest actor in the world.[5]

- Three-time Olympic gold medalist Ryan Murphy has a lot to celebrate. Not only is he an Olympic champion, but he also is the world record holder in the men's 100-meter backstroke. The 2016 U.S. Olympian proclaimed his Olympic goals when he was 8 years old in a picture he drew for his mother.[6]

- 2016 U.S. Olympian Morolake Akinosun forecasted her Olympic win in a tweet five years before her victory. She stated, "In 2016 I will be 22, graduated from a school I have not chosen yet, and going to the Olympics."[7]

DREAM BIG AND BELIEVE!

SHINE BRIGHT!

You were created to be comets, not to be common. Shine bright and make a huge positive impact!

AFFIRMATIONS TO SAY OUT LOUD DAILY

I am capable of doing difficult things.
I will always do the best I can.
I am a good listener.
I am perfect just the way I am.
I am a swift learner.
I am studious.
I have special gifts to share with the world.
Kindness is my super power.
I view challenges as opportunities for growth.
I am wise.
I remember things easily.
I enjoy helping others.

"Any idea, plan, or purpose may be placed in the mind through repetition of thought."
-Napoleon Hill
Self Help Guru

SUPERHEROES' LOG

"Vision + Action = Success"
-Rosanne Reid
International Best-Selling Author

A SPECIAL WORD FROM
KID UNI

Thanks for joining me! See you next time!

"Intelligence plus character --That is the goal of true education."

-Dr. Martin Luther King, Jr.
    Civil Rights Leader

ABOUT THE ILLUSTRATORS

A special thanks to all of the illustrators on this project, most of whom I met via social media. I'm most appreciative of the time and talent they shared on Volume One.

Eliran Malka, a native of Israel, is best known for bringing comic book Superhero 7 to the science world. His passion comes from his love of comic books and movies. Lately, he has been working on art for book covers and magazines using traditional drawing and digital painting (Cover page and Kid Uni). To see more of his current work, visit eli_sketchbook on Instagram.

Kiara Sanders is a 2017 graduate of North Carolina Central University's Art Department. Her preferred tools of the trade are acrylic paint, pencil, or her Wacom tablet. Outside of visual storytelling and illustrating, she is a recreational gamer, novice gardener, and follower of social issues ("Love" artwork).

Adair Carrol is a 13-year-old ninth grader who lives in North Carolina. She specializes in digital art using anime/manga art forms. Adair plans to be an animator and travel cross-country with her cats when she finishes school ("You Are Like Your Parents" artwork).

Adrei, is a 16-year-old talented graffiti artist from Dubai. Outside of spending time with his family and friends, he enjoys using his creative energy to design stunning murals. See more of his work at graffiti_dxb on Instagram ("Applying Words" artwork).

ABOUT THE ILLUSTRATORS

Declan McDowell is a 6-year-old student from St. Ann's Bay High and Preparatory School in Steer Town, St. Ann, Jamaica. He loves school, sports (especially football), singing and dancing, and drawing images from TV ("Magnetic M" artwork).

Lama Waleed is a 17-year-old Egyptian high school student living and studying in Saudi Arabia. She loves posting art on Instagram and horseback riding. Most of all, she enjoys seeking new challenges that allow her to uncover her hidden capabilities. See more of Lama's creations @young_artist on Instagram ("Shine Bright" artwork).

Garry Atkinson is an artist/illustrator who creates children's book through his publishing company, Fundo Press. His books, including "Fundo's Animal Alphabet," teach kids to learn through creativity. See more of his work at FundoPress.com and on Instagram @FundoPress (Layout Design and Digital Illustrations).

Interested in sharing your artistic talent in Volume Two? Let's connect on Instagram. Submit samples of artwork to @AggrandizeYourLife, #superheroesguide.

NOTES

1. David Creswell, Benefits of Self-Affirmation, Carnegie Mellon University, accessed August 19, 2017. http://www.cmu.edu/homepage/health/2013/summer/benefits-of-self-affirmation.shtml.

2. Brigid euroscientist: Meditation Not Only Reduces Stress, Here's How It Changes Your Brain," *Washington Post*, May 26, 2015, https://www.washingtonpost.com/news/inspired-life/w/2015/05/26/harvard-neuroscientist-meditation-not-only-reduces-stress-it-literally-changes-your-brain/?utm_term=.af782e58774f.

3. "Katy Perry," MusicMap, accessed August 19, 2017. https://www.musicmap.tv/interpret/katy-perry

4. "Visualization Is a Powerful Tool," *Men's Health*, January 16, 2013, http://forums.menshealth.com/topic/63643898169449330.

5. Jim Carrey, "Jim Carrey – Visualize, Believe, Manifest," September 7, 2016, YouTube video, 5:12, https://www.youtube.com/watch?v=oUUU6TQh64w

6. "Olympic Dream Realized: Ryan Murphy's Letter to His Parents About Being an Olympic Gold Medal Winner," Aired August 9, 2016, on *ABC World News Tonight.* http://abcnews.go.com/WNT/Video/Olympic-Dream-Realized-Ryan-Murphys-Letter-Parents-Olympic-41253745.

7. Doug Criss, "Runner's Tweet of Olympic Dreams Comes True," CNN, August 3, 2016, http://www.cnn.com/2016/08/03/us/morolake-akinosun-prediction-trnd/index.html.

ABOUT THE AUTHOR

San Griffin is a skilled professional in child development and family relations, with over 15 years of experience working with youth and their families. Upon receiving a bachelor's degree in child development and family relations and a masters degree in human development, both from North Carolina Central University, her mission was to educate, inspire and positively impact families around the world. Griffin, a wife and mother of three, takes this mission seriously.

As CEO of her brand, Aggrandize Your Life, LLC, Griffin uses her love of the brain and mind (neuroscience) to coach aspiring entrepreneurs to master their brains' creativity, emotions and productivity to reach their highest levels of success. The Aggrandize Your Life brand also offers early education workshops for adults approved for DHHS credit hours and entrepreneur and empowerment workshops for youth of all ages, in conjunction with school and college tours.

Connect with her at www.aggrandizeyourlife.com

AGGRANDIZE YOUR LIFE

Printed in the USA
CPSIA information can be obtained
at www.ICGtesting.com
LVHW051512021123
762343LV00004B/10